To the Reader:

I am grateful to meditate on God's wondrous works of creation with my family in our gardens and outdoor adventures and in my work as a Food Scientist. It is my life to know more and more about God through His Word, His Son Jesus, and His Creation. An aim of this book is to commend God's works to the next generation.

"One generation shall commend your works to another and shall declare your mighty acts." **Psalm 145:1.**

My experience taught me that not only the heavens but also butterflies and moths pour out God's speech day after day declaring that He created all things and that He is abundantly good and righteous. He is worthy of our praise and honor.

"The heavens declare the glory of God, and the sky above proclaims his handiwork. Day to day pours out speech, and night to night reveals knowledge. There is no speech, nor are there words, whose voice is not heard. Their voice goes out through all the earth, and their words to the end of the world." **Psalm 19:1-4.**

"On the glorious splendor of your majesty, and on your wondrous works, I will meditate. They shall speak of the might of your awesome deeds, and I will declare your greatness. They shall pour forth the fame of your abundant goodness and shall sing aloud of your righteousness." **Psalm 145:5-7.**

Neal and his wife Lida are grateful for their five children and two grandchildren (second to be born in 2017). They lived in MN, IL, MO, and now in CO. Neal serves as a Deacon at Reformation Church, OPC, in Elizabeth, CO. He has a Ph.D. in Food Science and worked as a Senior Principal Scientist in the Food Industry. He is grateful to study and photograph God's creation and learn connections with God's Word.

Front cover photo: Female Melissa Blue butterfly in our meadow in Elizabeth, Colorado. Notice the hairy white fringes on the wings. Collections of specialized hairs and nerves of butterflies sense the wind, temperature, and the position of the head, body, wings, legs, antennae, and other body parts. Butterflies are well equipped by an infinitely wise God to give Him glory! God blessed me with the sighting of another Female Melissa Blue butterfly in our meadow with unusual markings shown here. Apparently this is an example of genetic variation within a species. Watch my blog at creationspeech.com to see if I find another one like this in June.

Grey Glassy Tiger is a Milkweed butterfly similar to the Monarch butterfly

Copyright © 2017 by Neal A. Bringe

Published by CreationSpeech

ISBNs: 978-0-9984154-0-6 Printed Case
978-0-9984154-1-3 ePub
978-0-9984154-2-0 ePDF

Printed in the United States of America.

- God made everything in six days
- Nothing is too hard for the LORD
- God's eternal power and divine nature were clearly perceived since the creation of the world
- God will accomplish all He purposed
- God's works are wondrous. What other gods could do it?
- God is a spirit, infinite in His wisdom
- God's mercy is over all that He made
- God made vessels of wrath and vessels of mercy
- In Adam all die; in Christ shall all be made alive
- Whoever loves his life loses it, and whoever hates his life in this world will keep it for eternal life
- If anyone is in Christ, he is a new creation
- God is praised everywhere including the heights
- God will be exalted in the earth
- We have responsibility to rule over God's creation including every creeping thing
- Let the field exult the LORD and everything in it
- God can do all things. As we see His works we are humbled
- God gives His creatures food in due season
- God caused a world-wide flood and made a covenant to never do it again
- Do not be anxious. Seek God's kingdom
- The humble are the greatest in the kingdom of heaven

American Painted Lady on Zinnia flower

Dogface butterfly among wild Asters

"In six days the LORD made heaven and earth, the sea, and all that is in them, and rested the seventh day. Therefore the LORD blessed the Sabbath day and made it holy." Exodus 20:11

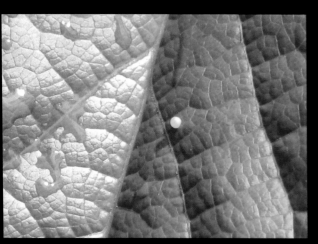

Living things are interdependent—each one needs another to exist. For example, while the male and female Zebra Swallowtail are needed to mate and produce a fertile egg, a Paw Paw tree is needed for the egg and caterpillars to survive. And, in order for the Paw Paw tree to live, beetles and flies are needed to pollinate the Paw Paw blossoms by transferring pollen from one tree to another in order to produce fruit with seed. Thus because God made these very diverse organisms during the same week: male and female butterflies, Paw Paw trees, beetles, and flies, they exist together in order to benefit each other and bring their Creator glory. We planted a Paw Paw tree in our yard to be able to see this beautiful butterfly. In God's providence, the one pictured blessed me with its presence on Father's Day.

Here is another example of interdependence. Yucca plants on our property in Colorado are dependent upon the Yucca moth. The pistil (green female part in the photo) of each flower ends in a three-lobed stigma. The female Yucca moth gathers pollen from the flower anthers (white parts) by using specially adapted mouth parts. Masses of pollen are formed into a ball by the moth and forced down into the central stigmatic hole enabling pollination and later formation of pods with seeds. The moth lays an egg in one or more of the chambers of the stigma so the caterpillar can feed on some of the seeds as a pod develops. According to the amazing plan of our Creator-God, the Yucca moth and plant depend on each other for their existence.

which specifically identify chemicals from Pipevine leaves.
...ter the vine grew on a trellis and we had an abundance
...and butterflies to enjoy. It seems that God has put these
...ationships in His creation to help us appreciate everything He
...f the Pipevine plant isn't nurtured, the Pipevine Swallowtail
...o longer exist to give God glory.

"For what can be known about God is plain to them, because God has shown it to them. For his invisible attributes, namely, his eternal power and divine nature have been clearly perceived, ever since the creation of the world, in the things that have been made. So they are without excuse." Romans 1:19-20

My wife, Lida and I were able to travel to Costa Rica and observe the butterflies (1991). The Morpho butterfly that I am holding in the picture shows a bright/glossy blue color. In part, the basis for this effect is rows of a precise structure within the scales of the wings that is only visible using an electron microscope. The distance between slits in the rows of structures corresponds to half of the wavelength of blue light. So waves of blue light reflect and align to create the iridescent color. In flight, the upper surface of the wings continually changes from bright blue to dull brown because the undersides of the wings are brown. My wife and I observed a Morpho butterfly in flight in the jungle. It seemed to disappear, and then reappear. This effect, combined with a wave-like flight up and down made the butterfly difficult to follow. The chrysalis (left photo) of another Costa Rican butterfly (Cream-spotted Tigerwing) appears as a jewel because of similar multiple thin layers that reflect back light. These wondrous works speak of the might of God's awesome deeds, His greatness and goodness.

"...I am God, and there is none like me, declaring the end from the beginning and from ancient times things not yet done, saying, 'My counsel shall stand, and I will accomplish all my purpose,' calling a bird of prey from the east, the man of my counsel from a far country. I have spoken, and I will bring it to pass; I have purposed, and I will do it." Isaiah 46:9b-11

Red Admiral

Hoary Comma

I was blessed to capture photos of Red Admiral and Hoary Comma butterflies with wings open and closed. Notice the intricate pattern of the underside of the wings. Isn't it amazing that a structure so thin has a different pattern on both sides of the wings? The butterflies can display bright colors or blend in with the surroundings as God purposed.

Female Eastern Tiger Swallowtail

Female on Zinnia

Black phase female on Iron Weed

God is in control of all things, including insects for His purposes. He can cause hornets to defeat an enemy of His people. He can also use His creation to encourage His people. God is the Father of mercies and God of all comfort (2 Corinthians 1:3). I remember the gift of seeing a female Eastern Tiger Swallowtail (upper two photos) in our front yard when I returned from the hospital after a surgery. It was an encouragement from a God who knows how I delight in His wondrous works.

followed a Cloudless Sulphur butterfly that was frantically flying around the yard until I saw it suddenly
op in our Persimmon tree. Otherwise, I would have never spotted it in the perfect hiding place (left photo)
Cloudless Sulphur showed this behavior again with another plant (right). Only God could create such c

God is a spirit, infinite, eternal, and unchangeable, in His being,
wisdom, power, holiness, justice, goodness, and truth."
From the Westminster Shorter Catechism (1647).

Red Spotted Purple

White Admiral

Viceroy

The Red-Spotted-Purple butterfly and Crab Apple trees are a wonder. The Crab Apple tree provides a dense display of bright blossoms in the Spring. The tree also is a food source for the caterpillar of the Red-Spotted Purple butterfly. According to God's plan, the adult butterfly is attracted to the trees, including the rotting fruit under the tree as a nutrient source; so, at the time when the tree is full of bright red apples, it is also graced by the butterfly. Notice how the patterns on the upper wing extend to the lower wing even though the wings are made separately. The White Admiral is a more northern form of the butterfly and can interbreed with the Red Spotted Purple. The Viceroy butterfly is similar and can interbreed. These butterflies represent an amazing variation within the same or similar species. With an infinitely wise God, all things are possible. His intricate creation tells us that He is worthy of honor.

"The LORD is good to all, and his mercy is over all that he has made."
Psalm 145:9

The Spicebush Swallowtail butterfly larva curls itself in the leaf of the Spicebush plant. God gave the larva this instinct to protect it from predators. God also shows his mercy by providing the larva with the ability to puff up the front of the body to look frightening, like the head of a snake. Furthermore, the caterpillar projects an orange appendage behind the head that has a strong offensive smell.

Butterfly and moth caterpillars typically go through four stages of growth as they molt their skin and become progressively more beautiful in appearance. This molting process is like our walk in Christ through the sanctifying work of the Holy Spirit. With each insight from God's word and the trials He ordains, we progress to a new level of understanding that helps us grow as we learn to trust Him more. Through it all God's patience and mercy are abundant and all-sufficient.

"What if God, desiring to show his wrath and to make known his power, has endured with much patience vessels of wrath prepared for destruction, in order to make known the riches of his glory for vessels of mercy, which he has prepared beforehand for glory." Romans 9:22-23

Polyphemus larva

White-lines sphinx larva

Luna moth larva

White-Lined Sphinx

Polyphemus

Luna

Glover   *(photo by Bob Fine)*

The above glorious moths seem only delightful. Even though the larva grow to a large size, usually no more than one egg is laid on a plant, so damage is minimal. In contrast, other moths eat vegetables (Tomato Hornworm) and others eat clothing. The Cabbage White butterfly larva eats Cabbage, Kale, Broccoli, Nasturtium, and the Black Swallowtail butterfly larva eats Parsley, potentially causing extensive losses in food production. These species are illustrative of the biblical principle of vessels of mercy and vessels of wrath. By common grace, God provides both with physical gifts and food.

Black Swallowtail laying eggs on Dill. Lower photo shows that there was little left of our Parsley because of the abundance of Black Swallowtail caterpillars.

> *"For as in Adam all die, so also in Christ shall all be made alive."*
> *1 Corinthians 15:22*

Pipevine Swallowtail

Black Swallowtail

Black-phase Tiger Swallowtail

Monarch

The above pictures show Swallowtail butterflies that survived bird attacks and a Monarch that was eaten. Maybe the tails and eyes of the hind wings of the Swallowtail butterflies helped to protect them as they provided a false head for birds to target. The reason that butterflies and their larva need protection is because of Adam's sin in the garden of Eden. The nature of God's creation after the fall of man illustrates the consequences of sin and the need for a Savior. The one who has overcome death and suffering is Jesus Christ.

"Truly, truly, I say to you, unless a grain of wheat falls into the earth and dies, it remains alone; but if it dies, it bears much fruit. Whoever loves his life loses it, and whoever hates his life in this world will keep it for eternal life. If anyone serves me [Jesus], he must follow me; and where I am, there will my servant be also. If anyone serves me, the Father will honor him." John 12:24-26

Monarch caterpillars feeding on milkweed

Monarch chrysalis

It seems that God made plants start as seeds, and butterflies start as caterpillars, to provide a purposeful picture, a living parable, illustrating that one must die to self to be transformed into a new creation that bears fruit for God.

"Therefore if anyone is in Christ, he is a new creation. The old has passed away; behold, the new has come." 2 Corinthians 5:17.

The beneficial transformations of a caterpillar into a chrysalis and a butterfly are miraculous, simply beyond our understanding. The same powerful God transforms persons from children of wrath (Eph. 2:3) to children of God. By the grace of God, a cursed person (Gal. 3:10), enslaved by wrong principles (Gal. 4:3-9) and passions of the flesh (Eph. 2:1-3), wholly unable to seek God (Rom. 3:10-12) is drawn by God (John 6:44), repents (Acts 26:20), comes to Christ and believes in Him (John 3:35) and becomes a new creation (2 Corth. 5:17), justified through faith in Christ (Gal. 2:16), a child of God (Rom. 8:16), living by the Spirit (Rom. 8:1-11, Gal. 5:16-26), who loves God and delights in his law (Psalm 1:2) and is progressively (Col. 3, 1 Thes. 5:23-24; Phil. 3:13-14) being trained by God (Phil. 2:12-13) to renounce worldly passions and live godly lives, zealous for good works (Titus 2:11-14), filled with hope in the return of Jesus Christ when body and soul will fully conform to His image (Rom. 8:29), enjoying God to all eternity (Rom. 6:22-23).

Monarch butterflies are made in a remarkable way to migrate from Canada and the Midwest U.S. in the fall, up to 2500 miles to a forest in Mexico, a place where predecessors were up to 3 generations ago, even to the same tree. The intelligent Creator who made this possible from the beginning of creation is God.

The butterflies above are members of the Brassy Ringlet group consisting of 10 species and 45 recognized subspecies found in fragmented alpine regions around the world. They were identified as forms of the Colorado Alpine and are similar to species in Siberia. The one on the right illustrates the metallic shine responsible for the name "brassy." Both of these butterflies were seen at about 10,600 feet elevation on a cold August day above Gardner Lake in the Beartooth Mountains, WY. Often at this elevation, caterpillars hibernate when they are still small. They develop further the following spring, forming a chrysalis sometime between June and August. A larva's persistence through winter is illustrative of how we should persist in patience and anticipation for the return of Christ. An explanation for how butterflies in this group can be found in mountains on both sides of the ocean is that the oceans were lower in the ice-age just after the worldwide flood, enabling plants and butterflies to distribute more easily around the earth. Earth is uniquely made for life through all its regions. Next page shows other butterflies seen at 8,000 - 13,000 feet elevation.

"Be still, and know that I am God . . . I will be exalted in the earth!" *Psalm 46:10*

Common Alpine

Rocky Mountain Parnassian

Melissa Arctic

Purplish Copper

Theano Alpine

Arctic Fritillary

Hoary Comma

Greenish Blue

Mormon Fritallary

Pale Swallowtail

Edith Checkerspot

Anise Swallowtail

Mead's Sulphur

Milbert's Tortiseshell

Let us make man in our image, according to our likeness; and let them rule over the fish of the sea and over the birds of the sky and over the cattle and over all the earth, and over every creeping thing that creeps on the earth." Genesis 1:26.

Planting tulip tree for butterfly and moth caterpillars

The wonders of a sphinx moth caterpillar

We have a responsibility to take care of God's creation including caterpillars, butterflies, and moths. One way we can do this is by growing and maintaining native plants. Our motivation is to love and honor God who made all things for His purposes in every environment. As a result, we are blessed. Children are captured by the wonders of creation and ask us many questions about it. As we explain our wonderful world to them, they will learn to admire and love the God Who thought of it all and included them in His plan.

"... sing to the LORD, all the earth! Sing to the LORD, bless his name; tell of his salvation from day to day. Declare his glory among the nations, his marvelous works among all the peoples! ...Worship the LORD in the splendor of holiness; tremble before him, all the earth! ... let the field exult, and everything in it ..."Psalm 96: 1b, 2-3, 9, 12a.

Green Hairstreak

Grey Hairstreak and Leafcutter bee

Melissa Blue

Common Wood Nymph

Where we live in Colorado, meadows are commonly mowed to limit weed growth. It is a humble task to manage noxious weeds (e.g., Mullen, thistles) of a meadow that is not mowed; but our efforts are richly rewarded as we observe a greater variety of plants and insects thrive, thus multiplying the glory God deserves by His reflection in the abundance of life.

"Then Job answered the LORD and said: I know that you can do all things, and that no purpose of yours can be thwarted ... I had heard of you by the hearing of the ear, but now my eye sees you; therefore I despise myself, and repent in dust and ashes." Job 42:1-2, 5-6

The Buckeye butterfly is strikingly beautiful to me and speaks to the majesty of God. We let our Oregano plants blossom because they attract this butterfly. There were many Buckeye butterflies around our home in Missouri when a field near us was filled with the broad-leafed Greater Plantain plant, a larval host plant. After treatment with broadleaf herbicide, the field became a solid plain of green grass, but no longer supported the regular viewing of the Buckeye butterfly. Maybe one could manage the field to have sections of meadow among the mowed grass areas.

"O LORD, how manifold are your works! In wisdom have you made them all; the earth is full of your creatures ...These all look to you, to give them their food in due season ...When you hide your face, they are dismayed."
Psalm 104:24, 27-29a.

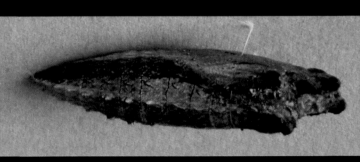

We are one of the means that God uses to provide food for His creatures. When the Canada Red Choke Cherry trees were planted in our front yard in Colorado they provided for the Two-Tailed Tiger Swallowtails. We are blessed to see them and learn from them. At any time God can take these blessings away from us. It is expected if we do not acknowledge Him and obey His Word.

"And God said to Noah, I have determined to make an end of all flesh, for the earth is filled with violence through them. Behold I will destroy them with the earth." Genesis 6:13

The rapid burial of creatures in the worldwide flood caused fossils to form. Caterpillars, bees, butterflies and dragonflies in the fossil record still look like the creatures that exist today. A private owner in Florissant, Colorado let me take a photo of the fossilized butterfly shown that is similar in appearance to the African Admiral. Another butterfly fossil was discovered in the same area that looks like the Snout butterfly along with a fossil of the larva food, Hackberry leaves.

Snout Butterfly

'Then God said to Noah and to his sons with him, 'Behold, I establish my covenant with you and your offspring after you, and with every living creature that is with you . . . I establish my covenant with you, that never again shall all flesh be cut off by the waters of the flood, and never again shall there be a flood to destroy the earth.' And God said, 'This is the sign of the covenant that I make between me and you and every living creature that is with you, for all future generations: I have set my bow in the cloud, and it shall be a sign of the covenant between me and the earth." Genesis 9:8-13

The rocks, fossils and rainbows are a witness to the truth of God's Word.

"He (Jesus) answered, "I tell you, if these (disciples) were silent, the very stones would cry out." Luke 19:40

And he said to his disciples, "Therefore I tell you, do not be anxious about your life, what you will eat, nor about your body, what you will put on. For life is more than food, and the body more than clothing. Consider the ravens: they neither sow nor reap, they have neither storehouse nor barn, and yet God feeds them. Of how much more value are you than the birds! ... Instead, seek his kingdom, and these things will be added to you. Fear not, little flock, for it is your Father's good pleasure to give you the kingdom." Luke 12:22-33.

We can observe how God provides for butterflies and moths and their caterpillars which are alive for a short time and then gone. How much more will he provide for his people who are made in His image and will live with Him forever. Seek His kingdom, walk humbly with God, enjoy His wondrous works and give Him glory.

> *"Let the children come to me; do not hinder them, for to such belongs the kingdom of God"*
> *Mark 10:14b*

The boys were excited to look for a Spicebush Swallowtail larva among the leaves when we got home from church. The photo on the right reveals what they found. The discovery was a speech poured out by God proclaiming that he exists. There is no end to knowing God. What a privilege that we can enjoy Him forever through faith in Jesus!